FAST FOOD

Written by Susannah Bradley

Illustrated by Cathy Hughes

Henderson Publishing

Woodbridge, England

INTRODUCTION

The recipes will be coded in the corner so that you can easily pick out those which are suitable for eating in certain places — these will include Breakfasts, Picnics, Parties, Things-to-slip-into-your-pocket-when-you-go-out-to-play, Saturday lunches, Tea times, Suppers to impress Mum, and Midnight feasts.

Breakfast **Teatimes**

Picnics **Saturday lunch**

Parties **Midnight Feasts**

Things to put in your pocket **Suppers to impress Mum**

The recipes themselves are in three sections:

Things to cook in the oven

Things to cook on rings and grill

No cooking at all

You need to be careful in the kitchen if you're going to live to taste these recipes, so take these simple precautions:

1. Tie long hair back before you start, so it can't get in the food or stop you from seeing what you're doing.

2. Protect your hands when touching something which might be hot — use oven gloves or something similar.

3. Never touch electrical points or gadgets with wet hands.

4. Keep pan handles turned where they cannot be knocked accidentally off the stove.

5. Never go away and leave something under the grill or on top of the stove while it is cooking.

6. Never turn on the gas without lighting it at once, and check that you have switched everything off as you finish with it.

7. Adult supervision may be required for some of the recipes.

WHAT TO DO IF THE CHIP PAN CATCHES FIRE

1. Turn off the heat, then soak a tea towel in water and throw it over the pan. Have another one ready in case this isn't enough.

2. If the fire persists, get everyone out of the house and ring the fire brigade from a neighbour's house.

COOK'S TRICKS

Here are some tips for making cooking easier.

Separating an Egg

Sometimes you need to use the white of an egg but not the yolk, or the other way round. When this happens, take two bowls and place them side by side. Tap the egg sharply on the rim of one of the bowls so that it breaks into two half-shells of equal size — but don't pull them sharply apart. Trap the yolk in one side, and let the white trickle into the bowl underneath.

Some of the white will be trapped in the half with the yolk in it, so rock the yolk into the other shell half and the remainder of the white will drip into the bowl.

Then drop the yolk into the second bowl

Peeling Tomatoes

It's horrible to find a stringy bit of tomato skin in a cooked dish, isn't it? They never go soft — so it's best to get rid of them before adding them to a dish. They are hard to remove before cooking, but if you drop them into boiling water for just one minute and then remove them from the water, you'll find that the skin will come off quite easily, although the tomato flesh is still firm enough for you to chop it up.

Making Shortcrust Pastry

The secret of making pastry is keeping it cool — so wash your hands in cold water before you start.

When you have to rub the fat into the flour, use only your fingertips and thumbs. Keep dropping the fat back into the flour and lifting and rubbing a different bit every few seconds — and when it has got to the 'breadcrumbs' stage, mix some cold water into it with a knife — never your fingers. Touch it as little as possible and you should have perfect pastry.

MOUSSAKA

This is a Greek dish, and you'll need aubergines for it. They are those purple vegetables which look something like long balloons.

300 g minced beef	Cooking oil
100 g onions	40 g plain flour
2 medium-sized aubergines	40 g butter or margarine
1 tablespoon tomato purée	300 ml milk
1 teaspoon ground cinnamon	50 g grated Cheddar cheese
Salt and pepper	1 egg
	40 ml water

1. Wash the aubergines and slice them into rounds which are 1 cm thick, throwing away the tops and tails. Put them into a colander and sprinkle salt on them, then put a small plate on top and weigh them down with something heavy like a bag of flour.

2. Peel and chop the onions and fry in some oil for three or four minutes. Then add the minced beef, tomato purée, cinnamon and 40 ml water.
Add some salt and pepper and leave it to simmer.

3. Heat two tablespoons of oil in another frying pan and fry the aubergine slices in it. They might need more oil to get all the slices covered, but be mean with it. Some will turn brown quicker than others; fish out the first ones to brown and put them in a layer on the bottom of a casserole dish and then turn the others off as they are cooked.

5. Now make the topping: Heat the butter or margarine in a saucepan, add the flour, and stir for one minute. Add the milk a bit at a time, stirring constantly. This is a white sauce; flavour it with the cheese, grated into it, and the salt and pepper. Turn off the heat, beat up an egg and add it to the sauce.

4. Put a layer of mince on top of the aubergines, then aubergines, then more mince, until everything's in the casserole dish.

6. Pour this topping over the meat and aubergine mixture in the casserole dish and cook it in the oven at Gas Mark 4/350F/180C for 40 minutes until the top has browned.

Meanwhile, do the washing-up!

Serves 4-6

BAKED APPLES

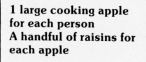

1 large cooking apple for each person A handful of raisins for each apple	A dessertspoon of soft brown sugar for each apple A little water Aluminium foil

1. Wash the apples.

2. Take the core out with a sharp kitchen knife or an apple corer.

3. Score a line around the skin halfway down the apple.

4. Place it on a big piece of foil and add a dessertspoon of water as you wrap up the apple. Do not press the foil against the apple — make it a loose parcel so that plenty of air can get in.

5. Before you do up the foil, stuff the centre with the raisins and brown sugar, mixed. Then finish sealing up the foil.

6. Cook for 40-50 minutes at Gas Mark 5/375F/190C.

BROWNIES

100 g butter	4 eggs
100 g plain chocolate	100 g ground almonds
100 g self-raising flour	Greaseproof paper
150 g sugar	

1. Put the butter and chocolate into a basin over a saucepan of boiling water. Leave it over the constantly boiling water until it melts.

2. Meanwhile, beat the eggs and sugar together until they are thick and light.

3. Mix the chocolate mixture into the eggs and sugar, and then fold in the flour and the ground almonds with a metal spoon.

4. Grease a Swiss roll tin and line it with well-greased greaseproof paper.

5. Pour the mixture on to this, and bake at Gas Mark 3/325F/170C for 40 minutes.

6. Turn it out and cut into squares.

Makes 12-16

CHEESE STRAWS

200 g plain flour (this can be plain, self-raising or wholemeal)	75 g grated cheese
	Pinch cayenne pepper
	1 egg yolk
100 g margarine	2 teaspoons cold water

1. Heat the oven to Gas Mark 4/350F/180C.

2. Put the flour into a big bowl and rub in the margarine between your fingers and thumbs so that it looks like breadcrumbs.

4. Beat up the egg yolk with the water and add enough of it to make a soft, but not sticky, dough.

3. Add the grated cheese and the cayenne pepper.

5. Roll it out on a floured surface. It should be about 6 cm thick.

6. Cut it into strips which are 6 cm wide and put the strips on to a floured baking sheet. Pop them into the oven and don't go away, because they'll only need five or six minutes to cook.

BAKED FISH

Cod cutlet	Pepper
Small knob of butter	A few frozen peas
1 tablespoon milk and water, mixed	You'll also need some aluminium foil

1. Cut a piece of foil large enough to wrap up the fish.

2. Place the fish on the dull side of the foil and add the pepper and the butter.

3. Add the frozen peas and the milk and water.

4. Do up the foil so that there is plenty of space inside the parcel to trap air in.

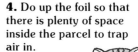

5. Put into the oven at Gas Mark 5/375F/190C for 20 minutes.

6. This goes well with jacket potatoes done in the oven at the same time, and baked apples. You can do them all in foil if you like — but don't forget what is in each parcel!

Serves 1

JACKET POTATOES

If you've only eaten these when they've been cooked in the microwave see how different they taste this way!

One large potato for each person Salt	Oil Filling (see below)

1. Set oven to Gas Mark 5/375F/190C.

2. Scrub the potatoes thoroughly but do not peel them. Then dry them with a piece of kitchen paper.

3. Put a little cooking oil into the palm of your hand and rub each potato with it. Then rub salt in on top of that. Wash your hands.

4. Put the potatoes on to a baking tray and cook for 1½ hours. It isn't fast food as it would be cooked in the microwave but it doesn't take long and you can be doing something else in the meantime.

5. Test to see if the potatoes are cooked by sticking a fork into them. The skins will be nice and crunchy — tasty, too.

Fillings:
Cut a big cross in the centre of each potato and push in from the sides so that it bursts open. Mash the inside with a fork and add:

OR: Don't make a cross in the centre — slice the top off, mash the inside and push it to the sides so that you have a hole in the centre. Then break an egg into the hole and put it back in the oven until the egg is cooked (about another 15 minutes).

Butter and grated cheese
Baked beans
Grated cheese and chutney

VICTORIA SANDWICH

This is the simplest sort of cake to make. You'll need two 16 cm sandwich tins to bake it in.

100 g butter or margarine	Vanilla essence
100 g castor sugar	Jam
100 g self-raising flour	Maybe some whipped
2 eggs	cream, too, if it's a special occasion

1. Heat the oven to Gas Mark 4/350F/180C.

2. Beat the butter or margarine in a mixing bowl with the sugar, using a wooden spoon or electric mixer.

3. Whisk the eggs and beat into the mixture, a little at a time.

4. Add three or four drops of vanilla essence.

5. Sift the flour into the mixture, holding the sieve high over the bowl so that lots of air gets mixed in too. Use a metal spoon to fold it through the mixture.

6. Grease the sandwich tins and dust with flour. Divide the mixture equally between the tins and smooth it out.

7. Bake on the centre shelf for 25-30 minutes. Don't open the oven door until 25 minutes are up. You'll be able to see if the cakes are cooked by pressing the centres lightly with your finger — if they spring back, they are cooked.

8. Take them out of the oven but leave them in the tins for ten minutes before easing them out of the tins onto the wire cooling tray.

9. When they are cold, sandwich them together with jam — or jam and whipped cream.

SCONES

Plain Scones

225 g plain flour	35 g butter or
4 level teaspoons	margarine
baking powder	Pinch of salt
25 g sugar	A little milk

1. Heat the oven to Gas Mark 7/450F/220C.

2. Sieve the flour into a bowl and add the salt and baking powder.

4. Stir in the sugar.

5. Add the milk in drops, stirring with a knife until it sticks together — but don't make it too sticky, or you won't be able to roll it out. If you're reading this saying "It's too late to tell me that now," then add more flour to stiffen it up again.

3. Rub in the butter or margarine between your fingers and thumbs so that it looks like breadcrumbs.

6. Roll it out so that it is as thick as your thumb and cut into rounds with a cutter.

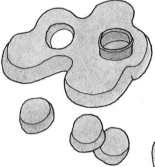

7. Put a little flour on to a baking tray and shake it from side to side until there is a thin film of flour all over it. Put the rounds on to this and bake for about ten minutes. You can test to see if they are done by pressing their sides; if cooked, they will be firm.

8. Split them open and fill with butter and jam — or whipped cream and jam.

Cheese Scones
Leave out the sugar and add 75 g grated cheese, extra salt, some pepper and dry mustard instead.

Wholemeal Scones
Use half wholemeal flour and half plain white flour. If you use all wholemeal they can be heavy.

JAMMY BUNS

200 g self-raising flour	¼ pint milk
50 g soft margarine	4 tablespoons red jam
50 g sugar	

1. Set the oven to Gas Mark 6 (200C, 400F).

2. Sift the flour into a mixing bowl. The reason you should sift it and not just bung it in is that sifting it adds air to it, which helps the texture.

3. Rub in the margarine. This means putting it in the bowl with the flour and rubbing it between your fingers and thumbs until it is so finely mixed with the flour that the two together look like breadcrumbs.

4. Add the sugar.

5. Drip in the milk, a bit at a time, stirring with a knife until it all joins up into a lump. You don't want a sticky mess, so if you think adding every drop of the milk will make this happen, don't add it, no matter what this recipe says.

6. Divide the lump into eight bits all the same size and knead them into balls.

8. Put some jam into each hole.

7. Grease a baking tray, put the dough balls on it, and make a hole in the middle of each with your thumb.

9. Bake for 15 to 20 minutes and then take them out and let them cool down before you eat them. Hot jam can badly burn you so don't be tempted to gobble one up before it has had a chance to cool!

SPAGHETTI BOLOGNESE

300 g minced beef
300 g tinned chopped tomatoes
1 green pepper
1 tablespoon tomato purée
1 medium onion

50 g mushrooms
1 teaspoon mixed herbs
1 teaspoon paprika
Salt and pepper
350 g spaghetti

1. Chop up the green pepper and the onion into small cubes. Put them into a saucepan with the minced beef, the tomatoes, tomato puree, mixed herbs, paprika and salt and pepper.

2. Heat the whole lot up together, stirring every so often to break up the minced beef and let the flavours mix in well. Soon they should be bubbling away; keep stirring regularly, and when it has been bubbling away for twenty minutes add the mushrooms, peeled and chopped up small.

3. Heat lots of water in a big saucepan and when it is boiling add some salt and the spaghetti. You will need to hold the sticks and curl them down into the water as they soften — and stir them while they boil to stop them sticking to each other and the pan. They will take ten minutes.

4. Then drain the spaghetti into a colander which you have placed in the sink — don't try to hold the colander or you could scald yourself with the water you pour away.

5. Put the spaghetti on plates with spoonfuls of the meat sauce over it. If you like, you can sprinkle some grated Parmesan cheese over it, but don't worry if you haven't any — it tastes very good as it is.

BOILED RICE

If you can boil rice so that it isn't a horrible gluey mess you will have the basis for many a tasty meal. You can add things to it like chopped peppers, nuts, peas and other vegetables, or serve it plain with stir-fries and other meat dishes.

Use **long grain rice** or **brown rice** with savoury dishes. **Short grain rice** is the kind needed for rice pudding!

For two people:

100 g uncooked brown or long grain rice **300 ml boiling water**	**10 g butter or 1 dessertspoon oil** **Salt**

1. Heat the oil or butter in a saucepan and stir the rice into it. Add the boiling water and salt. Stir just once, and then put the lid on the saucepan.

2. Turn the heat down as low as possible under the saucepan and leave it for exactly 15 minutes, if you are using white rice, or 35, for brown.

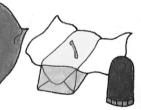

3. Turn off the heat, take off the lid, and serve it.

MACARONI MAIN DISH

150 g quick-cooking macaroni	75 gm grated cheese
1 onion, chopped	2 slices chopped ham
150 g tinned tomatoes	½ green pepper
	Salt

1. Put the onion and pepper in a saucepan of salted water and bring to the boil. When it is boiling, add the macaroni. Boil for seven minutes more, then drain off the water.

2. Put the tomatoes and a little of the juice into the saucepan with the onion and macaroni and replace on the stove over a gentle heat. Add the chopped ham and cheese and stir.

3. When the cheese has melted, serve in bowls and eat with crusty bread and butter.

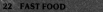

CHINESE STIR-FRY PORK

250 g pork fillet	2 courgettes
1 green pepper	1 teaspoon salt
2 carrots	1 teaspoon sherry
Some cauliflower florets	1 egg white
	1 teaspoon cornflour

1. First of all make a marinade with the salt, sherry, egg white and cornflour. (A marinade is a liquid in which the meat is soaked to make it tasty and tender.) Just beat all these things up together.

2. Using a chopping board and a sharp knife, cut the pork fillet into narrow strips about as long as your little finger. Put them into the marinade and leave them to soak while you prepare the vegetables.

3. Slice the green pepper into strips. Peel the carrots and cut them into strips, too. Do the same with the courgettes, cutting them into strips rather than round segments.

4. Cut the cauliflower florets up thinly.

5. Heat the oil in a wok or frying pan and drop the meat in for two minutes. Use a draining spoon to fish it out and leave it in a dish.

6. Pour most of the oil from the frying pan into a heatproof container and cook the vegetables in the little bit remaining in the frying pan or wok. Do not cook them for more than three minutes as they should be still rather crunchy when you eat them.

7. After the three minutes, add the meat and cook for a minute or two longer. Serve with boiled rice.

Serves 4-6

BEEFBURGERS

225 g best mince (some butchers call it minced steak) Salt and pepper	1 small onion, finely chopped A little Worcestershire sauce

1. Put everything into a bowl. You need only about six drops of Worcestershire sauce.

2. Mix it all up well together and then, with clean hands, shape bits of the mixture into round, flat cakes. Depending on how big you make them, you should end up with around six or eight.

3. Heat a little cooking oil in a frying pan and put the beefburgers into it.

4. Nudge them about a bit with a wooden spatula as they cook. They will need about ten minutes each side, but don't go away and leave them, because they could easily burn.

5. Be sure to keep the heat low, or the beefburgers will still be raw in the middle when they look cooked on the outside.

6. When you are sure that they are cooked right through (by slitting one with a knife, and peeping), drain them on kitchen paper, and serve them up . . . in a hamburger bread bun, or with a green salad, or both!

Serves 3-4

HOT DOGS

These are so simple to prepare! The secret lies in giving people a choice of what extras to put on them, so if you've got friends coming round, here are a few ideas.

Basic Hot Dogs

1. Tin Frankfurter or Hot Dog sausages
Long bread rolls — sometimes called bridge rolls

2. Put the sausages and the liquid which is in the tin (usually brine) into a saucepan and gently heat them.

3. Meanwhile, slit the rolls lengthways from top almost to bottom.

4. When the sausages are hot, lift them carefully out of the liquid and put them into the rolls. Don't stick a fork into them and try to haul them out — they will break if you do that. Use tongs if you have any, but otherwise nudge them, one by one, on to a draining spoon and lift them out that way.

Extras

Tomato ketchup — doesn't everyone have to have this on hot dogs?

Fried onion rings — slice the onion in cross-sections so that you have lots of round slices, and then push the layers apart before frying them lightly in a little oil.

Pickle — have several different sorts if you can . . . put them in little pots so that people can see to choose red pickle, brown pickle, green pickle, yellow pickle . . .

PAELLA

Have you eaten Paella in Spain? This is a simple version of it which is easy enough for inexperienced cooks to prepare.

Some cooked chicken (left over from a roast meal)	A green pepper
	Small tin chopped tomatoes
1 onion	2 tablespoons cooked peas
175 g brown rice	
Between 10 and 20 prawns (the frozen sort, thawed out)	2 pints chicken stock (make from stock cubes if you like)
A red pepper	2 tablespoons olive oil

1. Peel and chop the onion and peppers. Chop up the chicken into small pieces.

2. Gently heat the oil in a big frying pan and fry the chicken, onion and peppers in it until the onion is soft. Add half the stock and turn the heat down low so that it doesn't boil over.

3. After five minutes add the rest of the stock and the tomatoes and rice. Stir it well as you do so, but don't stir it much after that, or the rice could become sticky. After 15 minutes most of the liquid should have been absorbed into the rice. Add the cooked peas and the prawns, and cook for another five or ten minutes.

Serves 4

VEGETABLE SOUP

Any of the following:	Green Pepper
Onions	Turnip
Carrots	
Potatoes	You also need:
Leeks	A vegetable stock cube
Celery	Salt and pepper
Red Pepper	Water

When you have chopped all these vegetables up into very small pieces you bung-it-all-in a saucepan. The total weight of the vegetables used should be between 500 g and 750 g.

1. Make up the stock cube with 720 ml water. Pour this stock over the vegetables.

3. Cook for about 20 minutes, until everything is soft.

2. Bring to the boil, then add seasoning. Turn the heat down low.

Serve with lots of crusty bread.

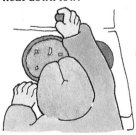

Serves 3-4

75 g red kidney beans	2 tablespoons cider vinegar
75 g haricot beans	½ teaspoon dry mustard
50 g fresh green beans (french beans)* chopped up	½ teaspoon sugar
50 g broad beans*	2 tablespoons mixed herbs
6 tablespoons olive oil	
Salt and pepper	

* Use frozen if French ones are out of season; if you can only find French beans, use twice as many and leave out the broad beans.

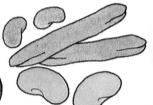

1. Boil the red kidney beans rapidly in plenty of water until they are soft. It is very important to keep them boiling, because undercooked beans are not good for you.

At the same time, cook the haricot beans in another saucepan of boiling water.

2. When both kinds of beans are cooked, drain the liquid from them and mix them together in a bowl. Use the saucepans to boil some more water and cook the french beans and broad beans for ten minutes or until just tender.

3. Put the oil, vinegar, mustard and sugar into a screw-top jar and shake them up well together.

4. Add the French and broad beans to the others and mix them together while they are still warm. Stir in dressing to taste from the jar, and chill before eating it.

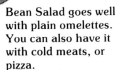

Bean Salad goes well with plain omelettes. You can also have it with cold meats, or pizza.

Basic Omelette

2 eggs 1 tablespoonful water Salt and pepper	A knob of butter or margarine

1. A small, non-stick frying pan is best for making omelettes in. You'll also need a spatula for poking the omelette with while its cooking.

2. Break the eggs into a bowl and beat with a whisk or fork. Add the water and a little salt and pepper.

3. Heat the butter or margarine in the saucepan but don't let it turn brown. Add the egg mixture. When it starts to set, use the spatula to push the sides of the omelette in towards the middle. Tilt the pan as you do it, so that runny egg from the centre runs out to make a new edge. Keep doing this all round the pan until all the egg is set. Fold it into three using the spatula, and slide it on to a plate to serve it.

It should be a mixture of brown and yellow on the underneath when you do this.

Variations:

Ham and Tomato: Drop a tomato into a saucepan of boiling water (not from a great height, or you may splash yourself) and take it out again with a serrated spoon after one minute. Let it cool down, and then you'll find that you can remove the skin quite easily, which you can't do when it's raw. Chop it up, and chop up half a slice of ham, too, and add them to the omelette mixture while it is cooking.

Cheese: Add some grated cheese to the omelette just before you fold it up. The heat from the omelette will make it melt.

Spanish Omelette: Have ready some cold boiled potatoes which you have cut up into small pieces. You'll also need some chopped onion, cooked gently in a little boiling water for five minutes so that they are quite soft. Add to the water some frozen peas as well. Drain and add to the omelette with the potato pieces as soon as you put the egg mixture into the pan. Serve flat.

> 1 egg for each person
> A little milk
> Salt and pepper
>
> A little butter or margarine

1. Break one egg for each person into a bowl. Add a tablespoon of milk for each egg and beat up with a fork or a whisk. Add a little salt and pepper. Heat the butter or margarine very gently in a saucepan on the stove. Add the egg mixture, and keep stirring until it thickens. Then serve it at once.

2. If you have a microwave oven you don't have to heat butter in a saucepan. You can cook the egg mixture in a bowl instead. Keep stirring it every few seconds. When it begins to thicken, take it out and serve it.

Variations:

Scrambled Eggs with Mushrooms: Gently fry some chopped mushrooms in the butter before you add the egg mixture. Don't let it burn, though!

Scrambled Eggs with Bacon: Grill some rashers of bacon and serve on top of the scrambled eggs.

Scrambled Eggs with Cheese: Add some grated cheese to the egg mixture before you cook it. Try some cream cheese instead for a mild, creamy flavour.

Spicy Scrambled Eggs: Add three or four drops of Tabasco sauce to the egg mixture. Don't be tempted to add more — you could find you've made it too hot for comfort!

Sometimes scrambled eggs are served on toast, but not always. They are just as good with brown bread and butter, or on top of a grilled potato waffle.

FRENCH TOAST

15 ml milk	15 ml cooking oil
2 eggs	2 tomatoes
2 thick slices of bread (wholemeal is best)	Salt and pepper

1. If you have a microwave you can cook the tomatoes in it. Cut them into slices and place them on a plate and put a piece of kitchen paper over them. Cook for 1 minute.

2. If you haven't got a microwave, put the sliced tomatoes under a hot grill for three or four minutes, with a little bit of margarine on each one.

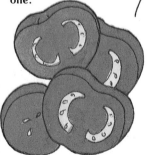

3. Break the eggs into a mixing bowl and beat them. Add the milk and some salt and pepper.

4. Heat the oil in a frying pan. Gently — don't burn it!

5. Soak the bread in the egg, then place it in the hot fat.

6. When the underside is brown, turn the bread over and cook the other side. This will take about two minutes for each side.

7. Serve it with the tomatoes on top.

Cheese on Toast

Slices of bread
Low-fat spread
Grated cheese

1. Make the toast first.
You can do this in a
toaster if you have one,
but if not, use the grill
pan. Toast the bread
lightly on each side, then
remove it from the grill.

2. Put some low-fat
spread on one side of the
toast and spread grated
cheese evenly on top.
Don't let any cheese
stick out over the sides
of the toast, but put
enough cheese on to the
toast so that all the toast
is covered. If you don't,
the bare patches will
burn.

3. Put it under the grill
until the cheese begins
to bubble.

Varieties:
Cheese and apple:
Finely dice some eating
apple, without taking off
the skin. Wash it first,
though! Add it to the
grated cheese.

Cheese and ham: Add
some chopped ham to
the grated cheese.

Cheese and tomato:
Use a serrated knife to
cut circular sections of
tomato. Place these on
top of the grated cheese
before you put it under
the grill.

**Two-tone Cheese on
Toast:** Grate two types
of cheese — Cheddar
and Red Leicester, for
instance, which are very
different in colour. Keep
them separate and put
them in stripes or like a
cross to make a pretty
pattern.

Egg on Toast

> Slice of bread
> Low-fat spread
> 1 egg

1. Have you got an egg poacher? If you have, poach the egg by heating some water in the pan and melting some low-fat spread in one of the little cups which fit into the top section, and then break the egg into this little cup. Put the lid on until it is cooked. It will take about two minutes. The water should be bubbling away underneath it all the time.

2. If you haven't got an egg poacher you will need a serrated spoon and a pan of boiling water. Break the egg into the water and wait until the transparent part turns white. Then hook it out of the water and put it on a slice of toast which you made before you poached the egg — if you leave it until afterwards you could find that the egg has gone hard with waiting.

An egg poached in water will cook more quickly than one done in a poacher, so be ready for it.

Variations:

Egg on Beans on Toast: Have some beans heating up while you are cooking the egg on toast. Put them on to the toast before you add the egg.

Peanut Butter Special: Make a piece of toast and spread it thickly with peanut butter. Add hot baked beans and a poached egg.

RASPBERRY ICE CREAM

| 450 g raspberries | 150 ml water |
| 175 g sugar | 275 ml double cream |

1. Wash the raspberries and mash them through a nylon sieve into a large bowl (you will have to do a few at a time until you've mashed them all.)

4. Bring it to the boil and boil for three minutes, and then pour it on to the mashed raspberries. Stir them up together.

2. Throw away the pips and stuff which is left in the sieve.

3. Put the sugar and water into a saucepan and heat gently, stirring all the time, until the sugar has dissolved (you'll know it has because you won't be able to see the sugar crystals any more).

5. Whip the cream until it is thick but not too stiff.

6. Fold it into the fruit mixture.

7. Pour it into a polythene carton and freeze for about three hours or until it has set round the edges. Then take it out of the freezer and pour it back into the bowl, and beat it up again.

8. Freeze it thoroughly this time, and eat it within a couple of weeks.

9. This recipe isn't exactly fast to make, but it counts as fast food because it disappears like magic when you serve it up!

Serves about 4-7 people (depending on how greedy they are!)

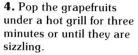

| Grapefruit | Ground ginger |
| Honey | Glacé cherries |

1. Cut each grapefruit in half.

4. Pop the grapefruits under a hot grill for three minutes or until they are sizzling.

2. Sprinkle a little ground ginger between your finger and thumb over each half.

5. Put half a glacé cherry into the centre of each one, and serve hot.

3. Swirl a little honey over the ginger in a thin spiral.

POPCORN

To do this you must have a heavy saucepan with a lid which fits well. Otherwise your kitchen could become a war zone as flying popcorn tries to whack you in the eye!

You can buy popcorn at the Health Food Shop. If you haven't seen it uncooked before, you will think that there isn't enough in the packet. There is; popcorn expands while it is cooking — you just wait and see how much!

> 50 g popcorn
> 1 tablespoon oil

1. Heat the oil in the saucepan.

2. Add the corn and put the lid on **straight away**.

3. Turn the heat down and wait. Within minutes you will hear loud popping noises. This is the popcorn splitting and turning inside out, bashing itself against the sides of the saucepan as it does so.

4. When it stops popping, turn off the heat and lift the lid. The popcorn will be ready to eat . . . unless you want to flavour it with . . .

Flavourings:
Maple syrup
(1 tablespoon is enough)
1 teaspoon curry powder
1 teaspoon salt
Honey and chopped nuts.

SANDWICHES

Ever tried triple decker sandwiches? Try using a mixture of breads — wholemeal top and bottom, and a slice of white in the middle. Fix them together with something different each side of the white — cheese and cress one side, tomato and mayonnaise the other, for example. Wholemeal is the best bread for sandwiches because it gives you fibre, protein, carbohydrates and several minerals. And if you use a low fat spread you'll be doing yourself a favour, too.

If your sandwiches are going to have to wait for you to be ready to eat them, choose a dry filling. If you can eat them straight away, choose anything you like. Strange how no one ever tells you that, so that you end up with a lunchbox of soggy, tomato-soaked sandwiches or a brownish mush of banana.

Sandwiches come in two sorts; doorsteps and dainty afternoon tea varieties.

Proper Sandwiches
Use sliced bread — it's quicker. Give each slice a scraping of low-fat spread, unless you're using something which is a spread in itself, like cream cheese, peanut butter or paté.

Do all one kind of filling at the same time, so you're not switching from one to the other all the time, getting jam in the fish paste and trying to pick cress out of the banana.

Slice a pile of sandwiches up together. They won't slip if you put the knife through the top one on the pile, and then press down on the pile with your spare hand as you press the knife through them.

Afternoon Tea For Great Aunts

The bread must be thin. You must cut the crusts off. The filling must be simple — paper-thin slices of cucumber, cream cheese and cress. Maybe honey if Auntie has a sweet tooth. You must cut them into little triangles and arrange them on a plate.

Filling Ideas

Grated cheese and pickle.
Honey and grated apple.
Mashed banana with powdered cinnamon.
Peanut butter and banana.
Tuna, mayonnaise and tomato ketchup.
Peanut butter and mustard and cress.
Taramasalata with hard-boiled egg rings.
Jam and natural yoghurt.
Cream cheese and pineapple chunks.
Red jam and pineapple chunks.
Cream cheese and cranberry sauce.
Grated cheese and apple slices.
Mandarin oranges and watercress.
Mashed avocado pear, lemon juice and prawns.
Frankfurter slices and tomato ketchup.
Cottage cheese with raspberries.
Lemon curd with flaked almonds.
Mayonnaise and peach slices.
Cream cheese and sweetcorn.
Mashed banana and raisins.
Ham, blackberries and banana.
Ham and mustard.
Peanut butter and sultanas.
Tuna, mayonnaise and celery.
Flaked crab, mayonnaise and tomato slices.
Roast beef and horseradish sauce.
Diced chicken, mayonnaise and cucumber.
Cold baked beans and sausage slices.
Sardines and tomato.

Green Salad

½ a lettuce	Celery sticks
¼ cucumber	Green eating apple
Cress	Chopped chives and
Watercress	parsley

1. Shred the lettuce into little pieces, using your hands.

2. Dice the cucumber and chop the celery finely.

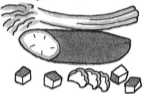

3. Wash the apple but do not peel it — cut it first into four, take out the core, and chop the rest up into thin slices.

4. Chop up the watercress.

5. Put them all into a big salad bowl and sprinkle cress on top. Just before you serve it, add a dressing like this one:

Salad Dressing
3 tablespoons oil
1 tablespoon vinegar
A pinch of dry mustard
A pinch of sugar
Salt and pepper

1. Shake all these things up together in a screw-topped jar. Don't pour it on the salad until the last minute or it will make everything soggy.

Mixed Salad

½ lettuce	1 tablespoon chopped nuts
¼ cucumber	Some pumpkin or sunflower seeds if you can get them
2 tomatoes	
½ red pepper	
½ green pepper	Celery
½ yellow pepper too, if you can get one!	1 eating apple
Cress	1 carrot

1. Chop the cucumber, celery and apple. Shred the lettuce. Cut the peppers into strips. Grate the carrot.

2. Put them all into a large bowl and add the tomatoes, quartered. Sprinkle with nuts, cress, and the sunflower and pumpkin seeds.

3. Serve with a salad dressing.

Coleslaw

½ small white cabbage
2 carrots
2 tablespoons mayonnaise
1 teaspoon vinegar
1 teaspoon oil
Salt and pepper

1. Shred the cabbage and carrot very finely. If you have a food processor you can shred them in that, but you can do it quite well with a knife . . . just mind your fingers.

2. Mix everything together in a bowl.

FRUIT SALAD

1 pear	1 banana
1 eating apple	A few strawberries
1 lemon	A few raspberries
1 orange	A little orange juice
1 peach	from a carton
Small bunch of grapes	Some cherries
1 kiwi fruit	A slice of melon
3 plums	

Note: Some of these fruits will not be in season, but it doesn't matter if you can't get everything, or if some of them have been frozen.

1. Peel the pear, the kiwi fruit, the orange, the plums, the peach and the banana and chop them up into small pieces, discarding the stones.

2. Wash the grapes and cut them in half, taking out the seeds if there are any.

3. Wash and stone the cherries, and cut small pieces of melon.

4. Wash the strawberries and raspberries.

5. Put everything into a big bowl and squeeze lemon juice over it. Add some orange juice.

6. Serve with cream or ice cream.

PITTA SNACKS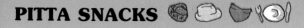

You can put hot or cold things inside pitta bread — warm it before you use it for the best taste. Pitta bread comes from Greece but you'll find it on the bread counter of most supermarkets.

1. Cut the pitta bread in half across the middle and you'll find that you can open it out like a little bag.

2. To warm it, put it under the grill, stick it in the toaster or the oven, if it's already on (it would be very wasteful of fuel to heat the oven just to warm up a pitta bread).

Open up the pocket and pop in:

1. Grilled bacon and tomatoes

2. Scrambled egg

3. Sausages and chutney

4. Cheese and Sandwich Spread

5. Tuna and tomato

6. Ham and baked beans

7. Grilled grapefruit seg - ments and honey

Iced Coffee

> 1 teaspoon instant coffee
> 300 ml cold milk
> 1 teaspoon drinking chocolate
> 2 teaspoons hot water
> 2 ice cubes
> 1 tablespoon whipped cream
> Sugar to taste

1. Mix the coffee and chocolate together with the hot water.

2. Whisk in the milk.

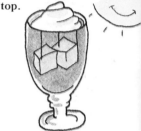

3. Add the ice cubes and float the cream on the top.

Ice lolly cubes

> Fruit juice or squash
> A few raspberries or slices of pineapple

1. Mix up the squash so that it is very strong — stronger than you would drink. Do not dilute the fruit juice.

2. Put a raspberry or small piece of pineapple into each section of an ice cube tray.

3. Fill up the sections with fruit juice or squash.

4. Freeze. When they are set, they can be sucked as ice lollies or put into drinks of the same flavour

SORE THROAT DRINKS

Hot Blackcurrant

> Concentrated
> blackcurrant drink
> 1/2 teaspoon mixed
> spice
> Boiling water

1. Put the blackcurrant into the bottom of a heatproof mug or tumbler. Add a little cold water.

2. Top up with boiling water.

3. Stir in the mixed spice.

Honey and Lemon

> A lemon
> A spoonful of honey
> Boiling water

1. Cut the lemon in half and squeeze all the juice into a cup.

2. Add boiling water to three-quarters of the way up the cup.

3. Stir in a spoonful of honey.

4. Top up with cold water so that it does not burn your mouth to drink it.